Antarctica

Lucy Bowman

Designed by Nicola Butler
and Josephine Thompson

Illustrated by Adam Stower
Reading consultant: Alison Kelly, Roehampton University
Antarctic consultant: Dr. John Shears, British Antarctic Survey

Contents

Down South

Antarctica is the most southern place on Earth. Most of the land is covered in thick ice and snow all the time.

Ice also floats on the sea. This is called an ice shelf.

A land of ice

Antarctica is the coldest and windiest place in the world. Most of the world's ice is in Antarctica.

It is so cold that every winter the sea around Antarctica turns to ice.

In summer some of the ice melts and rocky beaches appear by the sea.

There are dry valleys where no snow falls. They are the driest places on Earth.

Only the tallest mountains can poke through Antarctica's thick ice.

Crashing waves have carved this ice into a strange shape.

The wind is so strong in Antarctica that you can lean against it without falling over!

Icebergs ahead!

Icebergs are massive blocks of ice that break off ice shelves. They float in the sea around Antarctica.

This is the edge of an ice shelf. It has a huge crack in it.

The ice breaks away and the iceberg floats off.

This is the tip of an iceberg.
Most of the iceberg is hidden
under the water.

Icebergs come in many shapes and sizes.
Big icebergs are called ice islands. Small
icebergs are called bergy bits.

There are even bright green
icebergs, but scientists disagree
about why they are green.

Life on the ice

Scientists live in research stations in Antarctica. They study things such as the ice, animals and the weather.

These scientists are using a weather balloon to take measurements high up in the sky.

They weigh and measure young sea birds to check that they are healthy.

They collect lots of different rock samples to study back at the station.

Sometimes scientists travel away from their station and live in tents.

A piece of ice once broke off the ice shelf, carrying a research station.

Keeping warm

Scientists who work in Antarctica wear layers of clothes to keep them warm.

A scientist puts on a layer of thermal underclothes.

She then puts on a sweater, and thick socks and gloves.

The next layer is made of material that keeps out the wind.

She wears special boots and a warm hat.

In Antarctica, the sunlight bounces off the white snow. This scientist is wearing goggles to protect his eyes.

Crossing the ice

Scientists travel quickly from place to place on fast skidoos like the one below.

Skidoos slide over the ice on metal skis.

Food for the research stations arrives by ship. Strong ships called icebreakers clear a path for the supply ships through the ice.

The front of the icebreaker rises up over the ice.

It crashes down. Its weight breaks the thick ice.

The supply ship sails safely through the path in the ice.

Under the sea

Many different creatures live in the sea around Antarctica.

A krill is like a shrimp. Most birds and animals in Antarctica eat them.

Icefish have special blood that stops them from freezing in the icy water.

Antarctic sea spiders have tiny bodies and lots of long thin legs.

Colossal squids can be longer than two buses put end-to-end.

Some Antarctic jellyfish can be enormous.
This jellyfish eats small fish and krill.

This diver has
swum under
the ice to
take photos.

Pick of the penguins

Penguins live on the ice and in the sea.
Unlike most birds they cannot fly, but
they are very good swimmers.

These Adélie penguins are diving
into the sea to hunt for krill.

Penguins travel quickly on the ice
by sliding along on their bellies.

1. A mother emperor penguin lays an egg and gives it to the father penguin.

2. He keeps the egg warm in his pouch. She leaves to find food for herself.

3. The father penguins huddle in a group for warmth for over 60 days.

4. The egg hatches. The mother penguin comes back to care for the chick.

Blubbery beasts

Seals have lots of fat called blubber under their skin. It keeps them warm in the icy water.

These are Weddell seals.
They use their teeth to
make holes in the ice
so they can breathe.

Elephant seals are the biggest seals in Antarctica. The biggest and fiercest males are called bulls.

A young male seal moves toward a large bull.

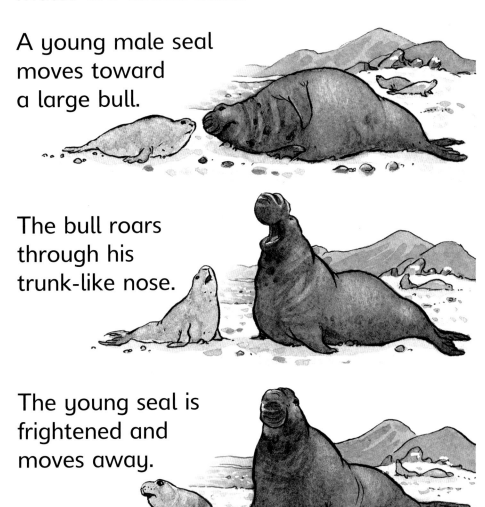

The bull roars through his trunk-like nose.

The young seal is frightened and moves away.

Giants of the deep

Thousands of whales go to Antarctica every summer to eat krill.

A humpback whale swims around and around the krill.

It blows air bubbles from its blowhole. The krill are trapped.

The whale swims up with its mouth open and catches the krill.

A blue whale can weigh
the same as 25 elephants.

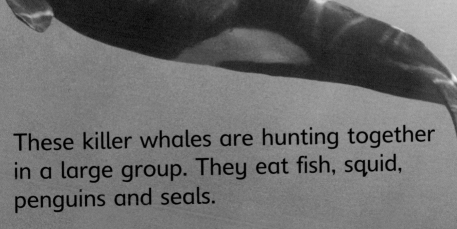

These killer whales are hunting together
in a large group. They eat fish, squid,
penguins and seals.

Soaring seabirds

Many birds fly to Antarctica every summer when there are lots of squid, fish and krill in the sea for them to eat.

This is a wandering albatross. It has very long wings and a sharp hooked beak.

Giant petrels are nicknamed 'stinkers' because of their horrible fishy smell.

Some seabirds like to eat other birds' eggs.

Snow petrels guard
their nests to keep their
eggs safe.

A skua tries to steal a
snow petrel's egg from
its nest.

The snow petrel spits
yellow oil at the skua
to scare it away.

Race for the Pole

The South Pole is the most southern place in Antarctica. In 1911, two teams of explorers, one from Norway and one from Britain, set out to find it.

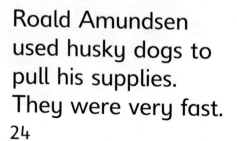

Roald Amundsen used husky dogs to pull his supplies. They were very fast.

Robert Scott went a different way and sent his dogs back to base camp.

This photo shows Scott's British team pulling heavy supplies and equipment.

Amundsen found the South Pole first. Scott found it one month later.

The weather turned much colder. Scott's team didn't survive the journey home.

Antarctic adventure

Sir Ernest Shackleton wanted to be the first person to travel from one side of Antarctica to the other. His journey began in 1914.

Shackleton and his crew sailed in a ship to Antarctica.

Before they could land, their ship was trapped in the ice.

This is a photo of Shackleton's ship trapped in the ice. It was called Endurance.

The ship was crushed and it sank. Some of the men sailed in lifeboats to find help, and the crew were rescued.

Good guests

Every year lots of tourists visit Antarctica. They must follow a set of rules to make sure they don't harm the wildlife.

Only 100 tourists from each ship are allowed on Antarctica at the same time.

They must not get too close to the birds and animals.

Tourists and scientists must take all their waste back home with them when they leave.

People follow these rules to make sure Antarctica is not spoiled.

Glossary of Antarctic words

Here are some of the words in this book you might not know. This page tells you what they mean.

 ice shelf - ice attached to Antarctica that floats on the sea.

 iceberg - a massive block of ice that has broken off an ice shelf.

 research station - a building where scientists live and do experiments.

 thermals - special clothing that traps heat and keeps the body warm.

 icebreaker - a strong ship that breaks through thick ice to clear a path.

 South Pole - the most southern place in Antarctica.

 husky dogs - fast dogs that pulled the first Antarctic explorers' equipment.

Websites to visit

You can visit exciting websites to find out more about Antarctica.

To visit these websites, go to the Usborne Quicklinks website at **www.usborne.com/quicklinks** Read the internet safety guidelines, and then type the keywords "**beginners antarctica**".

The websites are regularly reviewed and the links in Usborne Quicklinks are updated. However, Usborne Publishing is not responsible, and does not accept liability, for the content or availability of any website other than its own. We recommend that children are supervised while on the internet.

This picture shows the size of an iceberg above and below the water.

Index

Acknowledgements

Photographic manipulation by John Russell.

With thanks to Catriona Clarke.

Photo credits

The publishers are grateful to the following for permission to reproduce material:
© **Bettmann/CORBIS** 24-25 (Herbert G. Ponting); © **Bob Krist/CORBIS** 28-29 (Bob Krist);
© **Bryan and Cherry Alexander** 8, 12; © **CHRIS NEWBERT/Minden Pictures/FLPA** 20-21;
© **David Wall/Alamy** 22-23; © **Digital Vision** 6-7; © **Doug Allan/naturepl.com** 18;
© **Getty Images** 2-3 (Frank Krahmer), 4-5 (Ralph Lee Hopkins);
© **National Library of Australia** 26-27 (Frank Hurley); © **National Science Foundation** 11 (Josh Landis);
© **NORBERT WU/Minden Pictures/FLPA** 15; © **Ralph A. Clevenger/CORBIS** 31 (Ralph A. Clevenger);
© **Steve Bloom Images/Alamy** 1 (Pete Oxford/Steve Bloom Images); © **Tim Davis/CORBIS** cover, 16;
Every effort has been made to trace and acknowledge ownership of copyright. If any rights have
been omitted, the publishers offer to rectify this in any subsequent editions following notification.

Sun, moon and stars

Farm animals

Elizabeth I

Rubbish & Recycling

Dogs

Horses and ponies

Spiders

Planes

Cats

Ancient Greeks

VOLCANOES

DINOSAURS

Your Body

Armour

Sharks

The Celts

VIKINGS

Castles

How flowers grow

Digging up the past

Living in space

Caterpillars and Butterflies

Ballet

Pirates

Egyptians

Eggs and Chicks

ROMANS

Weather

Tadpoles and frogs

Why do we eat?

Under the sea

Bears

AZTECS

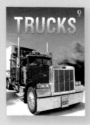
TRUCKS

Night Animals

Firefighters

Antarctica

Bugs

COWBOYS

Planet Earth

London

Seashore

China

Dangerous Animals

Rainforests

Trees

Reptiles

Ships

Bats

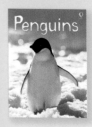
Penguins